Introduction to
GUITAR TONE & EFFECTS

2nd EDITION

An Essential Manual for Getting the Best
Sounds from Electric Guitars, Amplifiers,
Effect Pedals, and Digital Processors

By David M. Brewster

PLAYBACK+
Speed • Pitch • Balance • Loop

To access audio visit:
www.halleonard.com/mylibrary
Enter Code
"6718-3556-9467-8176"

ISBN 978-0-634-06046-5

HAL•LEONARD®

Visit Hal Leonard Online at
www.halleonard.com

Contact us:
Hal Leonard
7777 West Bluemound Road
Milwaukee, WI 53213
Email: info@halleonard.com

In Europe, contact:
Hal Leonard Europe Limited
42 Wigmore Street
Marylebone, London, W1U 2RN
Email: info@halleonardeurope.com

In Australia, contact:
Hal Leonard Australia Pty. Ltd.
4 Lentara Court
Cheltenham, Victoria, 3192 Australia
Email: info@halleonard.com.au

		Page	Tracks

INTRODUCTION

Welcome to the world of guitar effects and tone shaping. Since the earliest incarnations of electric guitars were produced, guitarists have strived to find a signature sound or original tone that would help set them apart from other players.

Jazz legend Wes Montgomery, for example, picked with his thumb and used a clean, bassy jazz tone to derive his own sound. Modern rock guitarist Mike Einziger of Incubus has adapted the use of various effect pedals and a semi-hollowbody electric guitar to create his own sound. Like most musicians, guitarists continually seek new ways to express themselves and often use novel and interesting tones to do so.

In this book, I'll introduce the equipment—electric guitars, amplifiers, various effect pedals, digital processing—and tones, sounds, and effects achieved by controlling and adjusting this equipment. As you progress through the book, listen to the accompanying audio examples of the effects and tones discussed.

Near the close of this book, you'll find a section entitled "Famous Effected Guitarists," which offers overviews on the setups of some well-known "tone-shapers," and the impact their innovative contributions have had on the use of amps and effects today.

In fact, it is the gifted imaginations of artists like these that have inspired the unique and amazing sounds that electric guitarists from every corner of the globe, and within every genre of music, utilize in creating their own new and exciting music.

Chapter 1
ANATOMY OF THE ELECTRIC GUITAR

Electric guitars come in all shapes and sizes, are constructed of different types of wood, and feature different electronics and pickup configurations. For many people new to the world of guitar, the multitude of options can be confusing.

Solidbody and Semi-Hollowbody Styles

Solidbody Guitars

The most common solidbody electric guitar style of today is based on Leo Fender's milestone creation: the Stratocaster. The first model to feature an integrated vibrato effect, as well as an ergonomically enhanced shape designed to facilitate playing, the Strat has been copied by nearly every guitar manufacturer since its introduction in 1954.

Fender Stratocaster

Because of its capability to produce a wide assortment of tones, the Strat-style electric is ideal for a number of music styles, including rock, pop, blues, funk, metal, country, and reggae. And its dedicated use by legends such as Jimi Hendrix, Eric Clapton, Buddy Guy, Stevie Ray Vaughan, Richie Blackmore, and Jeff Beck has helped to endear this solidbody to the hearts and minds of guitarists the world over.

Another popular solidbody guitar design is the Gibson Les Paul. Its revolutionary set-neck construction combined with the higher output humbucking pickups, which enhance sustain and provide a rich, warm tone, make it a logical choice for both rock and blues players.

Gibson Les Paul

Guitar legends such as Jimmy Page, Mick Taylor, Slash, and Warren Haynes favor the Gibson Les Paul.

Electric solidbody guitars can have almost any imaginable shape, and although the Stratocaster and the Les Paul are widely copied, there are other unique designs available and worth plugging into.

For example, another modern guitar design that is very popular today is made by Parker, a company that specializes in crafting unique-looking guitars with added custom features. Many Parker Fly guitars have piezo electronics built-in, which allow the blending of electric and acoustic tones together. The Fly fretboard is made of a composite material that gives it strength and produces a brilliantly resonate sound.

Parker Fly

Semi-Hollowbody Guitars
Semi-hollowbody (or semi-solidbody) guitars have an internal chamber that causes them to resonate much like a traditional acoustical guitar. When amplified, semi-hollowbodies produce a nice, warm tone, and tend to feedback more easily than regular solidbody guitars.

Gibson ES-335

Pioneered by the Gibson ES-335 model, other semi-hollowbodies are also available from Epiphone and Guild.

Guitar greats such as B.B. King, Ted Nugent, and Pat Metheny have been long-time proponents of these guitars.

Guitar Body Designs

Check out the following chart displaying different guitar body styles. Each will have varying degrees of impact on a guitar's producible tones.

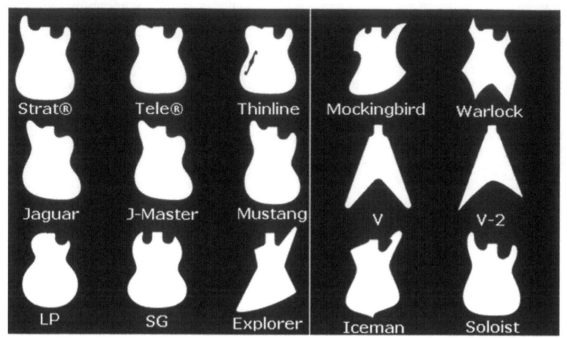

Various Body Designs

Headstocks

Another important factor to electric guitar tone is the headstock shape and design. Aside from the particular appearance it gives your guitar, the amount of wood and the angle of the headstock can affect the tone and sustain of your guitar.

The chart to the right illustrates some popular headstock designs. As the diagram shows, most Fender guitars have a "flat radius" headstock, which means that the area from the nut to the end of the headstock is straight or "flat." Gibson guitars, on the other hand (especially the Les Paul), have an "angled radius" headstock, which means that the headstock of the guitar is angled backward, thus improving the guitar's sustain and tuning stability.

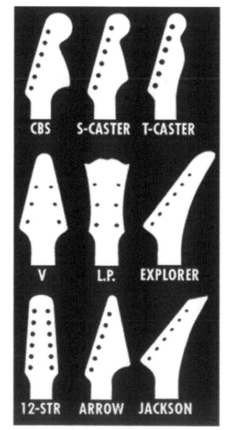

Various Headstock Designs

Body Construction

The following illustrates the look of some of the most common types of wood used for guitar body construction.

Common Guitar Woods

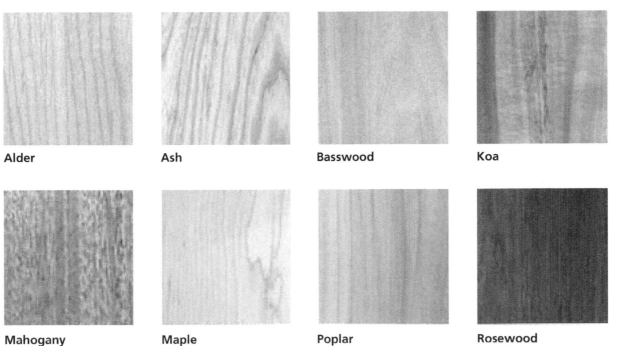

Alder   Ash   Basswood   Koa

Mahogany   Maple   Poplar   Rosewood

Different materials cause different tonal characteristics. Here is a rundown of weight and tonal quality by wood type:

- **Alder**—weight: light; tone: full and balanced. Plentiful and easy to work with, it is a common material for guitar bodies.
- **Ash**—weight: light; tone: warm and bright. Another popular wood. Fender has used ash in the construction of their Strat bodies for years.
- **Basswood**—weight: light; tone: warm.
- **Koa**—weight: medium; tone: warm and bright. Koa is an exotic wood generally considered too expensive to both manufacturer and buyer.
- **Mahogany**—weight: medium; tone: full with good sustain.
- **Maple**—weight: medium; tone: bright. Used to construct both bodies and fingerboards. Although there are a number of maple varieties available (i.e., birdseye, flamed, quilted), there are only slight differences in their tonal characteristics.
- **Poplar**—weight: light; tone: full.
- **Rosewood**—weight: heavy; tone: warm with less highs. It's most often used for fretboards, but occasionally used by some manufacturers for the entire guitar construction.

As the wood from which an electric guitar is made is very crucial to its function, some guitar manufacturers go so far as to select special grades of wood for their custom-made guitars, which explains why those models are usually more expensive and harder to come by.

Try to figure out what type of wood your guitar(s) is made from. If you're not sure, contact the manufacturer.

Pickups

Another factor that will alter an electric guitar's tone is its pickup(s). Pickups are electro-magnets wound with copper wire that, when soldered into the electronics of an electric guitar, sense the string vibrations as you play and send the signal that is eventually carried through your guitar cable and ultimately out of your amplifier.

Electric Guitar Pickups

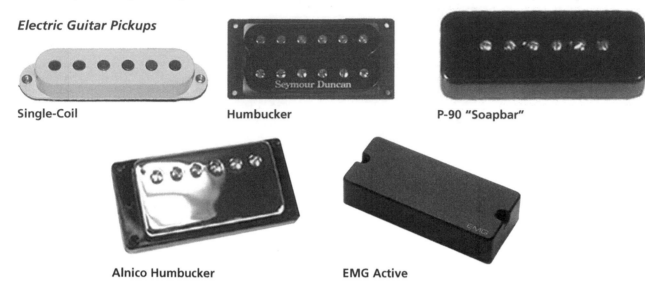

Single-Coil   **Humbucker**   **P-90 "Soapbar"**

Alnico Humbucker   **EMG Active**

Different pickup designs yield different results:

- **Single-coil pickups**—sound: thin. Subject to 60-cycle hum, which is interference with mics and electronic equipment.
- **Humbuckers**—sound: full with a rounder tone. No 60-cycle hum.
- **P-90 pickups**—sound: fuller than single-coiled pickups, but thinner than regular humbuckers.
- **Alnico humbuckers**—sound: full. Found on Les Paul-styled guitars.
- **Active pickups**—sound: high output and virtually noise free.

Replacement pickups for electric (and acoustic) guitars are available through manufacturers such as Seymour Duncan and DiMarzio. Their product lines feature various designs and options worth investigating. To ensure proper installation, replacing you electric guitar pickups should be handled only by an experienced technician.

Strings

Guitar strings are another important factor in getting a good guitar tone. Strings come in all different materials and sizes, and selecting the right string can help enhance your guitar sound.

Because electric guitars have electromagnetic pickups, their strings must have highly magnetic characteristics. Here are the most common materials used for electric guitar strings.

- **Stainless steel**—tone: brilliant. Anti-corrosive construction.
- **Nickel-plated steel**—tone: bright. Highly magnetic.
- **Pure nickel**—tone: more round and full than nickel-plated steel strings.
- **Coated strings**—improved tone, anti-corrosive protection for longer life (Elixer and D'Addario EXP brands).

The string gauge is important too.

- **Light**—tone: bright. Facilitate string bending and are easier on the fingertips.
- **Heavy**—tone: full and round. Better tone and sustain than lighter gauges.

The following lists gauge and corresponding tension level of each string when tuned to pitch:

	String						
	1st E	**2nd B**	**3rd G**	**4th D**	**5th A**	**6th E**	
Gauge	.008	.010	.015	.021	.030	.038	**Ultra Light**
Tension lbs	10.4	9.1	12.9	12.0	14.0	12.1	
Gauge	.009	.011	.016	.024	.032	.042	**Light**
Tension lbs	13.0	11.0	14.7	15.8	15.8	14.8	
Gauge	.010	.013	.017	.026	.036	.046	**Regular Light**
Tension lbs	16.2	15.4	16.6	18.2	19.2	17.1	
Gauge	.011	.014	.018	.028	.038	.049	**Regular**
Tension lbs	19.6	17.8	18.6	21.3	21.6	19.7	

Common String Gauges

The string gauge you use is ultimately a matter of personal taste. Guitar legend Stevie Ray Vaughan used very large strings (his high 'E' string was reportedly a .013). On the other hand, guitar giant Eddie Van Halen opted to use lighter strings (his high 'E' was a .009).

Plectrums/Picks

Guitar plectrums, or picks, can also play a factor in guitar tone. The following illustration shows an assortment of picks produced by Dunlop—the world's largest guitar pick manufacturer.

Assortment of Dunlop Picks

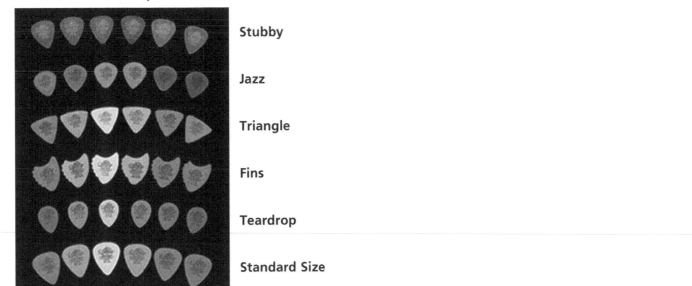

Stubby

Jazz

Triangle

Fins

Teardrop

Standard Size

Picks are made from a number of materials, such as Tortex (simulated tortoise shell), plastic, nylon, and even metal. Thumb picks, which are often used in country western and bluegrass music, contributed to the guitar tones of legends Merle Travis and Chet Atkins.

Some electric guitarists choose not to use picks at all, which helps them produce an altogether different tone when they are playing. Guitar legends Jeff Beck, Kevin Eubanks, and Robben Ford attack the strings of their guitar without the use of plectrums.

Thumb and Fingerpick

Chapter 2
CONTROLLING THE ELECTRIC GUITAR

Tone and Volume Controls

Take a good look at the controls on your electric guitar. If you are unfamiliar with their functions, now is the best time to learn what they are and how you can use them.

Tone and Volume Controls

Volume/Tone Knobs   Pickup Selector Switch

- **Volume knob**—adjusts the volume output of your guitar. (When not actively playing an amplified guitar, roll the volume knob to zero, so idle-string ringing or other annoying guitar handling noises won't be picked up and sent through your amp.)
- **Tone knob**—adjust the tone of your guitar to your liking.

Volume Control Knob

Tone Control Knob

Some guitarists constantly adjust these controls while playing, while others seem to "set it and forget it," rarely adjusting or touching the controls at all. For our purposes, the volume and tone settings of your guitar should be set at their maximums ("on 10," "cranked," "wide open").

Pickup Selector

The pickup selector switch allows you to change between the pickups outfitted in your guitar. Some guitars only have one pickup, while others have several. Guitar guru Steve Morse has outfitted his custom guitars with four single-coil and humbucking pickups.

Such a setup is illustrated in the following diagram. This example of five-way pickup selection switching shows the different pickup combinations that are activated simply by moving the switch. While Position 1 typically produces a sound that is bright and snappy, Position 5 typically sounds warm and bassy. As you move the switch around, you'll hear audible differences ranging from "glassy" to "beefy."

Five-Way Pickup Selector Switching

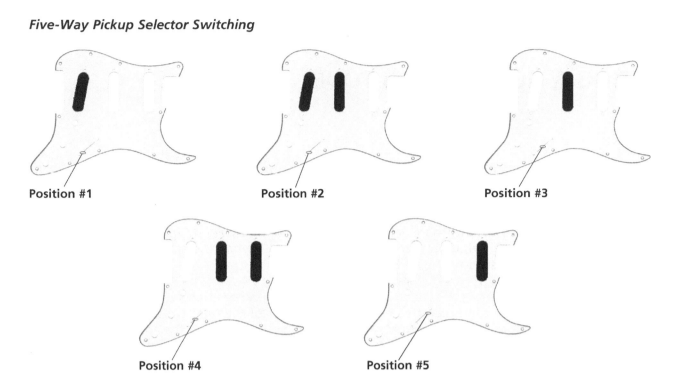

Position #1   Position #2   Position #3

Position #4   Position #5

If, however, your guitar only has two pickups, the following diagram demonstrates the selections for a three-way switching system.

Three-Way Pickup Selector Switching

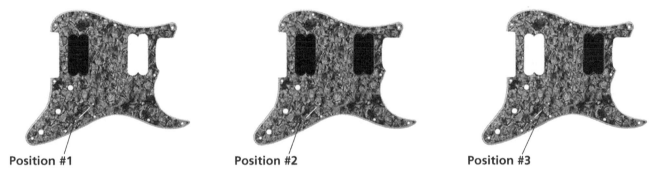

Position #1   Position #2   Position #3

This particular pickup configuration is quite common and represents the pickup combinations of any two-pickup guitar (such as a Les Paul). The following guide describes the qualities of the three positions:

- **Bridge position**—sound: bright and thick. Especially good for overdrive and distortion.
- **Middle position**—sound: thinner and trebly. Sounds good when mixed with bridge or neck pickups. It is commonly heard with rhythm playing and clean tones.
- **Neck position**—sound: warm and bassy. Common for overdriven leads and clean tones.

Once you are comfortable changing the volume, tone, and pickup settings on your guitar, you might want to listen a little more carefully to your favorite guitarists. Certain tonal characteristics are obvious once you have spent enough time listening to the subtle tonal variances that occur when players alter their controls.

Chapter 3
GETTING A GOOD, CLEAN TONE

In this chapter, we'll discuss the perfect way to begin searching for your own signature sound. But before you attempt to use any effects or tone-shaping devices, you must dial in a flat-response clean tone on the amplifier that you'll be using.

I'm positive that most guitarists out there actually use amplifiers that were designed for guitarists (a guitar amp). But did you know that some guitarists prefer to use keyboard amplifiers or even bass amplifiers to help them achieve pristine and pure, clean tones? It's true!

The reason it's crucial to attain a pure, clean tone prior to adding other effects to your signal is for better overall tonality. If you can find a clean-sounding amplifier of the right wattage and size for you, then anything that you add to the signal path (between your guitar and the amplifier's natural sound) should accentuate what your natural electrified-guitar tone sounds like. Simply put, if your amplifier sounds good when plugged directly into your amp, anything additional should only improve the sound.

The Step-by-Step Process
If you find that a new effect pedal or processor that you've purchased sounds funny or downright bad through your amp, you may need to find something else to use, or you may need to follow these guidelines to get the desired results:

Step 1—Start from Scratch
The best way to start is by unplugging any pedals, processors, equalizers, compressors, and the like from your amplifier. Be sure that you start with only your guitar plugged straight into your amplifier. This might be hard for you to do, but trust me; this is the first step to remedying a bad or undesirable guitar tone.

Once unplugged, you are ready to familiarize yourself with the features and functions of your amplifier.

Step 2—Know Your Amplifier
Although there are countless guitar amplifier manufacturers and hundreds (if not thousands) of different amplifier models, styles, and sizes on the market, their overall layout is pretty much the same. Whether a combo (self-contained) amplifier, or a head-and-cabinet design, the basic layout and description of the amp controls should be somewhat similar. The following illustrations show some of the differences found in two popular combo guitar amps.

Combo Guitar Amplifiers

Amplifiers feature different speaker sizes: normally 10-inch or 12-inch, unless it is a small practice amplifier, which could have a 6- or 8-inch speaker. The main distinction between speakers of different size is the area through which the sound can vibrate. Smaller speakers mean less room for vibration and handle smaller sound waves (high end, or high frequencies), whereas larger speakers (i.e., 12-inch or 15-inch) have more surface area and thus handle larger sound waves (low end, or bass frequencies).

One or two 12-inch speakers are normally sufficient for an at-home guitarist, but many performing guitarists prefer the louder and fuller sound of having four 12-inch speakers in their cabinet. Both the full-stack (two 4" x 12" cabinets and amplifier head), and the half-stack (one 4" x 12" cabinet and amplifier head) are quite common setups for the performing musician. And aside from the visual impression a larger amplifier system makes, its capability for louder volume levels can be essential when playing large auditoriums or concert halls.

Half-Stack Amplifiers

Another important factor of guitar amps is wattage—the power rating of the amplifier—and should be considered before buying an amp. Some guitarists insist on having 100-watt amplifiers, while others prefer 50-watts or less.

If you plan to play your guitar primarily at home, you may want to opt for a smaller amplifier with less wattage. On the other hand, if you plan to perform live with a band, you may need more stage volume and power.

The following are some of the various names manufacturers assign to an amplifier's controls:

- **Gain control**—a.k.a. saturation, overdrive, or distortion. Adds overdrive or distortion to your amplifier's tone.
- **Master knob**—a.k.a. master volume, or volume. Does exactly what you might think: controls the overall volume level selection for your amplifier.
- **Equalization controls**—add or reduce the amount of low, middle, and high range frequencies in your guitar amp's tone. Too much of any of these controls might make your guitar amp sound "trashy," "harsh," or downright ugly.

The following are illustrations of typical one- and two-channeled amplifier panels. Compare these to your amp. Which do you use?

Single-Channel Amplifier Controls

Two-Channel Amplifier Controls

Step 3—Set Your Amp's EQ to "Flat"

Now that you have identified the type of amplifier you are using (single- or two-channeled amplifier), you should set your amplifier to its cleanest (non-overdrive) sound. To do so, turn any gain, overdrive and reverb controls to their minimal or zero settings, and adjust the EQ controls to a flat response (12 o'clock). Once you have done this, turn your master volume control all the way off (zero).

Twelve o'clock EQ Settings (Treble, Mid, Bass)

Now, plug your guitar into your amplifier and turn on your amp. Decide what volume you would like to set your amplifier to. Be considerate to housemates and neighbors when making this choice. Also, playing amplified at loud volumes without the protection of earplugs for long periods can cause ear fatigue and lead to gradual or even sudden hearing loss. Be careful!

By playing through and adjusting your amplifier at a lower volume, you may discover new settings that you prefer over what you'd used at a louder volume. But also keep in mind that, at either low or high volume levels, your amp's sound will be influenced by the size of the room in which you're testing your amp, the number and size of your amp's speakers, and your amp's circuitry (tube or solid-state).

It's usually believed that tube amplifiers sound better when stressed (played at louder volumes), but this is not always the case. Many solid-state amplifiers sound relatively the same at their minimal or maximal settings.

Step 4—Set Your Amp Accordingly

Now that you have set your amplifier on a clean setting and have decided on your volume level, you should perform a few things on your amplified guitar. Listen carefully; pay close attention to the response that your guitar and amp have when they are used together like this.

In this next step, decide on what EQ changes you'd like to make. Does it sound a bit trebly, or is there too much low end? Getting the mid-range frequencies set properly at this point is very important, because the mid-range frequencies will accentuate the high and low frequencies.

The following illustration shows a typical EQ setting configuration for getting a good, balanced, clean sound.

Suggested Clean Amplifier Setting

It's important to notice in the illustration that none of the controls are turned above 12 o'clock. The reason for this is so your amplifier won't create unnatural brightness, lowness, or overdrive/distortion, and most guitarists want to attain a more mellow-sounding guitar tone. However, you may find that the 12 o'clock setting is exactly what you want; use your own judgment.

Now that you have listened to your amplifier at different settings, continue tweaking until you reach a balanced, clean guitar tone.

Chapter 4
OVERDRIVE, DISTORTION, AND FUZZ

The "overdriven" or distorted amplifier sound is the one most sought after by guitarists of almost every musical style. Finding the right amount of overdrive or distortion can accentuate the guitarist's chords, riffs, and solos. For example, the normally smooth and warm sound of a clean tube amplifier can turn into a "buttery" overdrive sound when the amp is overpowered with sheer volume and high output pickups (such as the humbucker).

In the early days of rock 'n' roll, guitarists such as Scotty Moore (Elvis Presley) and Chuck Berry were known for their slightly overdriven tube amplifier sounds, which they got by turning the master volume of their amps beyond the normal listening position.

In the '60s, groups such as The Kinks ("You Really Got Me", "All Day and All of the Night") found creative ways to produce more "grit" and drive. Guitarist Dave Davies has reportedly cut small slits into his amp's speaker with a razor blade to help him achieve a nastier and more "abusive-sounding" overdrive.

Overdrive
The first step in tailoring a good-sounding overdrive tone is to choose between the built-in overdrive from your amplifier (if applicable) or a floor pedal (stomp box).

🔊 Listen to audio track 1 to hear an example of the overdrive sound.

TRACK 1

Built-in Overdrive
Many tube amplifiers have built-in overdrive, but many older models (or re-issues) are predominantly clean with only a slight hint of overdrive. Most solid-state amplifiers feature high levels of gain (a.k.a. overdrive) that you can adjust to a moderate setting if you wish to use your amp's built-in overdrive. Tube amplifiers, on the other hand, will "break up," or achieve natural overdrive, due to the transformers, tubes, and circuitry contained within. Solid-state amplifiers rely on additional circuitry and electronics to achieve overdrive.

Following are examples of typical overdrive settings for a few common musical styles:

Blues and Country

Suggested Amp Overdrive Settings for Blues and Country Guitar

This illustration shows the starting point for a getting the slightly overdriven sound commonly heard in blues and country music. Of course, there are variations of overdrive heard within these genres and different settings used to get them. For example, to get a clean, B.B. King-type tone, use less gain; to attain a modern-blues, Kenny Wayne Sheppard-type tone, use more gain.

Rock

Suggested Overdrive Amp Settings for Rock Guitar

The above shows typical settings used to attain a solid rock guitar tone. For a classic rock sound, "beef up" this tone with a little more gain.

Metal

Suggested Overdrive Amp Settings for Metal Guitar

The EQ setting shown here is called "scooped mids," which means most (or all) of the mid-range frequencies are reduced—the typical characteristic of a metal guitar tone.

Floor Pedals

If you have decided to use a floor pedal or "stomp box" to achieve overdrive, compare your pedal with the following illustration—a classic Ibanez overdrive pedal.

Ibanez Tube Screamer Overdrive Pedal

This is what a typical overdrive pedal looks like. The level control adjusts its overall volume, the tone control adjusts its overall EQ frequencies, and the drive control adjusts the amount of overdrive. (Remember that the overdrive output of the pedal will add to your amp's overdrive signal.)

The Ibanez Tube Screamer was made famous by Stevie Ray Vaughan, who actually used two of these pedals in his guitar rig. This pedal is commonly used as a "boost," to increase the overall volume level and add sustain, but it is not used for massive amounts of overdrive.

In addition to your amp's built-in overdrive (if applicable), using overdrive pedals will "beef up" the sound of your amplifier, "fatten" your tone when soloing, or "dirty up" your rhythm parts.

Try the following overdrive pedal settings typical for the these musical genres:

Suggested Pedal Overdrive Settings:

Blues and Country Guitar

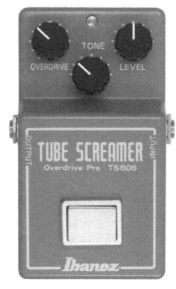

Rock Guitar

Metal Guitar

Distortion

Distortion produces a level of overdrive that is more edgy and intense. It's common to all types of metal music, as heard in the early metal of groups such as Black Sabbath, through the modern sounds of bands like Lamb of God.

The easiest way to produce good-sounding distortion is to use either a foot pedal, a solid-state amplifier, or a preamp/processor that features a distortion effect. Tailoring the EQ is crucial in achieving the tonal results you're looking for.

Many metal guitarists use additional equalization for their metal tone. The late guitar great Dimebag Darrell has reportedly added parametric EQs to shape his brutal tone.

 Listen to audio track 2 for an example of distortion.

TRACK 2

If your amplifier has built-in distortion, you may not need a distortion pedal or processor. The amount of distortion your amp is capable of producing will be determined by its model type and style.

If you want more or a different distortion than what you get when configuring your amp's controls to the suggested settings shown for metal guitar in the previous chapter, then you'll need to find a good distortion pedal.

This classic BOSS DS-1 distortion pedal can be found in many famous guitar rigs. Guitarists such as Joe Satriani and Steve Vai have included this pedal in their arsenal of stomp boxes. There are many brands of distortion pedals on the market; I suggest trying out as many as possible to find the one(s) that best fits your needs.

Boss DS-1 Distortion Pedal

Fuzz

Fuzz guitar tones fall somewhere between overdrive and distortion and have a syrupy, stinging tone quality. Guitar legend Jimi Hendrix turned the world onto the cool overdrive tones that fuzz pedals produce. Other notable fuzz users are Eric Clapton (during his Cream days), Eric Johnson, Robin Trower, and Eddie Hazel (of Parliament).

 Listen to audio track 3 for an example of a fuzz tone.

TRACK 3

This is the fuzz pedal model used by legends such as Jimi Hendrix and Eric Clapton.

Vintage fuzz pedals are hot commodities, and the rare ones usually fetch big dollars at guitar shows, in music stores, and on Internet auction sites.

Now that you have a better understanding of how overdrive, distortion, and fuzz effects can alter and enhance your basic guitar tone, I would recommend that you spend time with any (or all) of these tone-shaping effects and try to emulate the sounds of your favorite guitarists.

Dallas-Arbiter Fuzz Face Fuzz Pedal

Chapter 5
EQUALIZERS

Now that you have created a good clean tone and experimented with different types of overdrive and distortion, you should learn more about what equalization is and how you can use it to further adjust and enhance your tone.

The two types of EQs that will be explained here are the graphic EQ and parametric EQ.

Graphic EQ
A graphic EQ is normally equipped with small faders (or sliders) aligned across select frequencies, which, when individually adjusted, combine to shape the *overall* sound or tone of an audio signal (i.e., a PA system, guitar amplifier, bass amplifier, etc.)

The following illustration shows a basic 6-band graphic EQ pedal:

The layout of a typical graphic EQ pedal is very similar to a rack-mounted graphic EQ. The faders can be manipulated and moved to boost or reduce the particular frequencies found in your signal.

EQs can tailor your guitar tone by eliminating unwanted frequencies or boosting the desired frequencies that your amplifier is insufficiently creating. An EQ can also be used to boost your guitar's output level, which is useful when an increased volume level is needed for guitar solos or musical interludes.

MXR Six-Band Graphic EQ Pedal

Here we see a typical rack-mountable EQ:

Behringer Ultra-Graph Pro Rack-Mountable Multiband EQ

The appearance of the rack-mountable EQ is similar to the foot pedal EQ, but it is housed in a tabletop or rack casing. Graphic EQs such as the Ultra-Graph Pro will provide even more tonal variety, and they are available in 15, 20, or even 31-band models.

The best way to begin working with graphic EQ settings is simply to experiment with different fader settings. Once you've got your signal running a graphic EQ, sustain a chord on your guitar and slowly begin to move the faders around, adding or removing certain frequencies. Listen carefully to what this does to your overall guitar tone.

Parametric EQ

Parametric EQs are common for players wanting to accentuate their amplifier's tone, eliminate feedback, or just incorporate different frequencies into their sound.

Normally, parametric EQs feature dials for the manipulation of signal frequencies, rather than the faders found on graphic EQs. Most parametric equalizers on the market have frequency-selective filters, which allow for precise changes in overall tone. Usually these filters control the low, mid, high-mid, and high ranges of frequency in an audio signal.

 Listen to the audio track 4 to hear the manipulation of a distorted tone using a parametric EQ.

TRACK 4

Chapter 6
COMPRESSORS AND LIMITERS

Most musicians are aware that guitarists of all styles have been incorporating compressors and limiters into their guitar rigs for decades, but many are confused by what these two useful effects actually do and the differences between them. Compression reduces or boosts uneven signal levels to help create a balanced and even-sounding guitar tone. A limiter cuts the signal at a specified threshold peak, leaving the original tone unchanged.

Compression
Compression for guitar may not be as noticeable as other effects. It's not about what it will change in your tone, but about how it will control the overall volume, sustain, attack, and "feel" while you're playing.

 Listen to audio track 5 to hear a guitar riff played first without compression, and then with compression.

TRACK 5

The following illustration shows the layout of a typical compressor pedal.

**Boss Compression Sustainer CS-3
Compression Pedal**

The level control adjusts the volume, and the tone control adjusts the overall tone of the compression effect. The attack control is for managing the effect's application of compression to your signal; but by placing this at a higher setting, it can also improve the response and feel when you are playing. Likewise, setting the sustain control higher can add additional sustain to your signal and give your tone a balanced feel and sound.

Once you have incorporated a compressor to your guitar signal, you should learn more about how to set and its controls. The images on the next page illustrate the common settings for smooth and balanced compression.

Suggested Compression Settings:

Smooth Compression   **Balanced Compression**

Be sure to perform chordal and lead work when setting up your compressor, as it will affect how your guitar and amplifier respond when played.

There are several brands of compression pedals and rack-mountable units available. A feature of many rack-mounted units is more flexibility or control over the compression effect. But for a crash course in what compression can do for you, I suggest investing in a foot pedal first.

Chapter 7
NOISE REDUCTION

Guitar amplifiers, effect pedals, single-coil pickups, fluorescent lighting, faulty patch cables, poor guitar wiring, or unbalanced amplifier and effect parameters can contribute to a noisy guitar signal. Although usually attributed to the pickups in your guitar, the hum that normally accompanies a guitarist's amp and equipment—the 60-cycle hum—can also be caused by any or all of the above-mentioned factors.

Several units on the market can help a guitarist control the amount noise produced by their rig. These products—normally called noise suppressors or noise gates—can help you quiet the hissing sounds that multiple effect pedals, long patch cables, and other noisy rig elements are notorious for.

 Listen to audio track 6 to hear the transparent effect of a noise suppressor on a guitar signal; first without noise suppression, and with suppression added.

TRACK 6

Noise Gate
The following illustration shows a popular noise reduction pedal.

Rocktron Guitar Silencer Noise Reduction Effects Pedal

Chapter 8
MODULATION EFFECTS

Modulation effects seem to go hand-in-hand with guitar rigs. Whether by way of pedals or rack systems, some of the biggest names in guitar playing have incorporated modulation effects into their sound.

This chapter will feature a brief overview of each modulation effect. The accompanying audio tracks will help you identify the sound of each effect by demonstrating a performance first without the effect, and then with the effect added.

Chorus
Using a chorus effect at a moderate setting will not only add depth to your overall sound, but will simulate a "doubling" effect, sounding as though two or three guitarists are playing simultaneously with you.

 Listen to audio track 7 for an example of the chorus effect.

TRACK 7

The following illustrates a basic chorus pedal.

Boss Chorus CE-2 Chorus Pedal

The rate control, as shown in the illustration, modulates chorusing speed, and the depth control adjusts the range of the chorus effect.

Try one of these suggested settings for a smooth or clean chorus sound:

Suggested Chorus Settings:

Smooth Vintage Chorus   **Spacious, Clean-Tone Chorus**

The more time you spend with this effect, the more you'll realize its importance to the guitarist. You may not want to use chorus all the time, but for some tones (clean, or lead and rhythm parts), this effect can be invaluable.

Phaser

TRACK 8

The phase effect featured on audio track 8 is similar to that heard on the recordings of many famous guitarists. In fact, it seemed that everyone was phaser crazy in the seventies; not only guitarists used them, but drummers, vocalists, and bass players alike.

One of the most famous "phase-crazed" guitarists is Eddie Van Halen. Eddie used a phaser during much of his early work with Van Halen, and many of his most memorable leads and rhythms had a slight touch of phase applied to them.

The phase effect has a gradual "sweep" when adjusted at a moderate setting. It can also be very interesting when its controls are set higher, producing a tone reminiscent of a rotary speaker.

Guitarists will sometimes use a phaser as a tone filter, which changes the tonality of the guitar sound. Most prefer the phaser's smooth and "swooshing" effect to other modulation effects.

The following illustration shows the layout for a classic phase pedal.

The controls on most phasers are similar to that of the chorus pedal: a speed control, and an intensity control to manipulate the depth of the effect.

MXR Phase 100 Phase Pedal

Check out these useful settings:

Suggested Phaser Settings:

Early Van Halen Phase Effect

"Buttery" Phase Effect

Flanger

The flanger is the twisted relative of the chorus and phaser effects. Because it rotates a portion of the sound in and out of phase with another portion, which varies the delay time, it produces a "swampy," or churning type of sound. Flanger is ideal for guitarists looking for something more obnoxious than chorusing or phasing.

Listen to audio track 9 to hear an example of the flange effect.

TRACK 9

Much like the phaser, the flange effect can be heard in plenty of popular music and found its way onto many recordings of the 1970s. One of the most popular flanged guitar recordings is the classic song "Barracuda" by the classic rock band Heart. Its thunderous intro riff and piscatorial theme are accented perfectly by the menacing, slippery flange effect heard throughout the tune.

The following illustrates the control layout for a classic flange pedal.

The controls for a flange effect are quite different from that of a chorus or phase unit. The manual control knob adjusts the overall "feel" of the effect; the speed knob controls the speed, or rate of delay; the width knob manipulates the degree of the effect; and the regeneration control can widen the effect's range, and also produce "metallic" tones.

It is important to experiment with any effect pedal or device, but you should plan on investing a little extra time to get a useable sound from your flanger. This effect can be a bit hard to control when set beyond minimal settings, as it tends to colorize and blur the original guitar tone.

MXR Flanger Pedal

The following illustrates some useful flange settings.

Suggested Flange Settings:

Moderate Flange Effect   **Wild Flange Effect**

Tremolo

The tremolo effect is reminiscent of the sound common to the classic guitar amps of the 1950s and 1960s. While its sound is somewhat similar to the flange's watery tone, the tremolo produces an even more pronounced underwater effect. Its warbling, shaking sound can be heard in all types of music, from blues and rock, to country and jazz.

 Listen to audio track 10 to hear an example of the tremolo effect.

TRACK 10

Check out the following illustration, which shows the layout for a typical tremolo pedal.

Boss TR-2 Tremolo Pedal

Vibrato

The use of vibrato became quite common after Jimi Hendrix was heard using it. Many popular guitarists from the 1960s used the Uni-Vibe vibrato pedal, which produces a "buttery," swirling sound.

Some guitarists confuse vibrato and tremolo, but these two effects produce audibly different results. Listen to audio track 11 to hear the vibrato effect. Listen once again to the tremolo on audio track 10 to distinguish the difference between the two sounds.

TRACK 11

Numerous manufactures produce vibrato pedals, and most multi-effect processors feature this useful modulation effect. Dunlop makes a replica of the Uni-Vibe, as well as a similar product called the Roto-Vibe, which is an all-in-one foot-controlled vibe unit.

Vibrato is still used by guitarists today and can be heard in the music of guitarists such as Robin Trower, Warren Haynes, and Kenny Wayne Sheppard.

The following illustration shows a popular vibrato pedal.

The controls of most vibrato pedals are similar to that of phase pedals: the intensity knob controls the degree of the effect, and the speed knob controls the rate of vibrato.

Modulation effects can change your guitar signal dramatically and color your sound in unique and unexpected ways. Spend some time listening to each modulation effect demonstrated on its accompanying track, and then decide for yourself which of these effects are right for you.

Voodoo Labs Micro Vibe Vibrato Pedal

Chapter 9
REVERB AND DELAY

Both reverb and delay are effects that can add acoustical "space" and dimension to your guitar and amp tone. Their characteristics are quite different and are applicable to a number of different styles.

Reverb
The reverb effect produces the sensation that you're listening to your amplifier in a large hall or acoustical chamber. Processed reverb has been utilized for years and is typically applied to all instruments in recording studio situations.

 Listen to audio track 12 to hear an example of the reverb effect.

TRACK 12

Vocalists and instrumentalists have taken advantage of the natural reverb of concert hall acoustics since the days of Gregorian chants and early chamber music. The constructors of opera houses further exploited sonic reverberation, designing them with the intent of capturing its natural qualities for the improvement of tone projection.

Today musicians and sound/studio engineers collectively spend millions on high-dollar rack units and processing gear in order to perfect the quality and clarity of their reverb signals.

Most guitar amplifiers have built-in reverb, which is caused by the vibration of a large, coiled spring set within an internal "reverb tank." If you have reverb built into your amplifier, you may have heard the coiled spring rattle when your amp is turned up, or when your live amplifier has been jolted or knocked over. Usually the reverb on an amplifier is controlled by one knob; the higher you set the knob, the more the effect will be mixed in with your original signal.

Some amplifiers don't feature built-in reverb, but don't worry; there are plenty of products out there that can give you this effect. There are foot pedals and effect processors that can produce great-sounding reverb. Invest some time in finding one that works best for you.

Most rack-mounted reverb units offer more control over the reverb type and the management of variables (such as the room size). Also, pre-delay and reverb decay are usually adjustable with these units.

Reverb is a very functional and valuable effect that can give a small and wimpy guitar tone a surge of power and depth.

Delay
The delay effect is also commonly found in guitarists' set-ups and can provide a number of useful sounds and tones. A delay device samples the input signal and then plays it back after a specified amount of time. It can produce an echo-type effect, or if set for longer delay times, can allow you to harmonize guitar parts with yourself.

 Listen to an example of the delay effect found on audio track 13.

TRACK 13

Some of the most notable delay users include Brian May (Queen), Eddie Van Halen, David Gilmour (Pink Floyd), Albert Lee, Steve Vai, and The Edge (U2).

Check out this illustration of a popular delay pedal.

Boss Digital Delay DD-6 Pedal

The controls for a delay pedal such as this are as follows: the level adjusts the delay's volume level; the feedback (or repeat) knob adjusts the number of delayed repeats; and time control sets the duration of time between echoes or repeats.

The delay will allow you to simulate various repeating effects. A minimal setting will produce "slap-back," which offsets whatever you are playing by milliseconds. The slap-back effect is especially common in country music, but has been used by many famous guitarists in various musical styles.

Setting the delayed signal for a longer interval can produce some interesting effects as well. Pink Floyd's David Gilmour used delay on the classic tune "Run Like Hell."

Play around with these suggested delay settings:

Suggested Delay Settings:

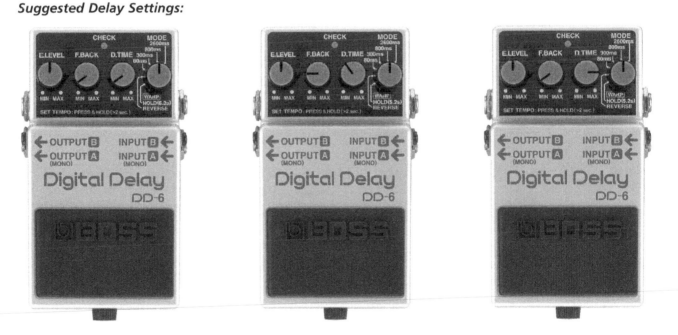

Slap-Back Effect   **Moderate Delay Effect**   **Long Delay Effect**

These sample settings would be a good place to start your experimentation with this effect. You should also set these controls at various settings to see what sounds you can produce.

If you're using a rack-mounted or floor-based multi-effect processor, the control settings illustrated above can be translated accordingly, but keep in mind that many delay devices have a number of variables and settings that are important to understand.

A typical delay processor measures its effect in milliseconds (500 milliseconds being equivalent to half of a second). Many delay pedals or processors also limit the amount of delay producible—some can go to 500 milliseconds, others to 700 milliseconds, while a few can sample and repeat the delayed signal in full seconds.

Chapter 10
OCTAVERS AND HARMONIZERS

Octave Effect

Octavers, or octave dividers, fatten guitar tone by producing additional notes an octave above or below the note played. Some octavers can even stretch the pitch spectrum up to two octaves.

 Listen to an example of an octave effect on audio track 14.

TRACK 14

Octavers have long been a favored effect by many guitar legends, including as Jimi Hendrix, who used the popular Octavia model, which was built especially for him by effect guru, Roger Mayer.

The following illustration shows a popular octaver pedal.

The control layout for this pedal is simple: the level control adjusts the overall effect level, and the octave 1 and 2 knobs control the "blend" between the original signal and the additionally produced pitches.

Boss Octave OC-2 Octaver Pedal

Harmonizer

Like octavers, harmonizers have been in use for years, and this sound effect has been tapped into by many great guitarists—Steve Vai, Brian May, Trevor Rabin, just to name a few. It's not uncommon to find expensive rack-mounted harmonizers (such as an Eventide) in modern guitar rigs.

Where an octaver can produce an additional, octave-spaced tone, a harmonizer offers a larger selection of intervals to add to your sound. In addition to octaves, they are capable of creating fourths, fifths, and other intervals.

Conventional and Intelligent Pitch Shifters

There are two main types of harmonizers on the market: a conventional pitch shifter, and an intelligent pitch shifter. Listen to audio track 15 for an example of the harmonizer effect.

TRACK 15

Conventional pitch shifting delivers harmony based on a preset interval range; in other words, if you set a conventional pitch shifter to "fifths," it will perform intervals of fifths, whether it sounds good or not with what you are playing.

Intelligent pitch shifting performs harmony by automatically detecting the pitch you're playing and incorporating the interval structure appropriate to and in tune with that.

There are several brands and models of rack-mounted harmonizers on the market, and many can be very expensive. Check out this illustration of a high-end harmonizer unit used by some of the guitarists mentioned on the previous page.

Eventide Ultra-Harmonizer H3000 Rack-Mountable Effect Unit

Chapter 11
SPECIAL EFFECTS

In this chapter, we'll cover special effects designed to create unique and innovative sounds. Some effect pedals and processors are one-of-a-kind; many are even fervently sought after by musicians and collectors, as such effects help guitarists create unnatural and unusual sounds—a potential "signature" for many guitarists.

Wah Pedal

The wah pedal is probably the most popular guitar effect. It's a foot-controlled tone potentiometer quite similar to the tone pots found on electric guitars. Moving the foot pedal back and forth adjusts the tonal balance of the instrument's signal (the wah is used not only by guitarists, but bassists and keyboardists as well), causing the sound to distort in a way implied by the effect's name.

 Audio track 16 features example of the wah effect's sound.

TRACK 16

Famous guitarists from various musical styles—from Eric Clapton to Steve Vai—have found new and exciting applications for this versatile effect. Icon Jimi Hendrix made many guitarists' jaws drop upon first hearing the sound captured on his landmark recording "Voodoo Chile (Slight Return)." The wah manipulation, which lends to the sheer, rocking funkiness of this cut, still sounds fresh some fourty-plus years later.

The following illustration shows a very popular wah pedal.

Dunlop Cry Baby 535Q Multi-Wah Pedal

Envelope Filter

Envelope filters allow wah-styled effects without necessitating the manipulation of a pedal with your foot. Once the effect is turned on, the pedal (or processor) will automatically "sweep" wah-like effects.

 Listen to audio track 17 to hear an example of an envelope filter effect.

TRACK 17

Although envelope filters doesn't exactly duplicate a real wah-pedal sound, they are useful—especially if you're seeking a "freaky" and interesting sound—and can be found in many rock and funk guitar rigs.

The following is an illustration of a popular envelope filter pedal.

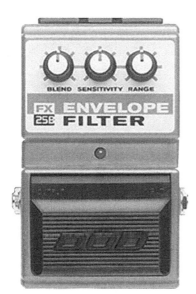

The control layout for an envelope filter is as follows: The blend knob controls the degree to which the original (unaffected) signal filtered effect blends. The sensitivity control adjusts sensitivity level of the effect in response to your pick attack (as this effect can react differently to hard and soft picking techniques). The range knob controls the overall depth of the effect.

DOD FX25B Envelope Filter Pedal

Talk Box

The Talk Box was an extremely popular effect upon its introduction in the early 1970s, and despite its dated technology, is still heard on newer recordings today. The effect itself is quite interesting: it's comprised of a long plastic tube, which is inserted into the effect user's mouth, and through which sound travels to the effects "box." When the user "talks," the mouth movements and voicings manipulate and project the sound through the tube, which shapes the chord or note struck on the guitar.

 Listen to audio track 18 to hear an example of a Talk Box effect.

TRACK 18

The most famous user of this effect is probably Peter Frampton, who on his glorious 1976 live album, *Frampton Comes Alive*, asked via a Talk Box, "Do you feel like I do?" Other notable Talk Box guitarists are Joe Perry and Joe Walsh.

Dunlop Heil Talk Box

NOTE: You won't be able to hear this effect simply by hooking it directly into your guitar amp—you'll need some additional equipment. Connect a microphone to a PA system to hear the effect in action. The microphone will amplify the effect through the sound system, allowing you to hear yourself "talk" with your guitar.

Pitch Shifting

In addition to duplicating the effects of an octaver (one or two octaves), a pitch shifter also performs pitch bends, harmony shifts, and greatly expands overall note range. Its most recognizable capability is probably the whammy effect, which simulates the "dive bombing" sound of the locking Floyd Rose tremolo.

 Listen to audio track 19 to hear an example of a pitch shifter.

TRACK 19

While there are a few rack-mounted units on the market, most pitch shifters are activated by a foot pedal (like a wah pedal).

Famous pitch-shifting guitarists are Dimebag Darrell (Pantera), Tom Morello (Rage Against The Machine), and Joe Satriani.

The following is an illustration of a very popular pitch shifter, DigiTech's Whammy.

Controls on the Whammy include a preset for dive bombs, mechanical momentary switch, and interval selectors.

DigiTech Whammy Pedal

Acoustic Simulator

The final special effect featured in this chapter is quite interesting. As its name implies, an acoustic simulator shapes an electric guitar sound to that of an acoustic.

Many acoustic simulators do this task quite well, changing the tonal spectrum and EQ of an electric guitar so that it sounds thinner and brighter—much like a plugged-in acoustic-electric (rather than a non-amplified steel-string acoustic).

 Listen to audio track 20 to hear an example of an acoustic simulator effect.

TRACK 20

Normally, acoustic simulators are manufactured in pedal form, but they can be found in effect processors too. The following illustration shows a popular acoustic simulator pedal.

The pictured model features four distinct selectable modes for simulating a variety of acoustic guitar sounds and tones, and is footswitch-activated/deactivated. It is an interesting effect if you want to add acoustic sound capability to your electric guitar rig.

Boss Acoustic Simulator AC-2 Pedal

Chapter 12
COMBINING EFFECTS

Now that you're familiar with some of the most common guitar effects and their sounds, you should learn how to arrange them for the best sound possible.

Whether you are using foot pedals, rack units, or processors, their placement within the signal chain is crucial to your overall sound. The following diagram lists the effects covered in this book in their proper order. Whether you are using one or all of these effects, follow the sequence of this signal chain, ignoring those effects you're not using in your rig.

Effect Signal Chain

Use this diagram as reference whenever you're unsure about effect placement.

In actuality, it may not be realistic to run this many individual pedals at once with your rig, as such a set-up would be quite noisy. As a result, the noise gate would have to be at a higher than normal setting, and be activated every time you weren't playing—otherwise the hiss from the pedals would be deafening. A better option would be to take a minimalist's approach with effects pedals and try to get the best possible sound from your amplifier before incorporating additional signals to your tone.

Look over some of the suggestions in this chapter, which will help you decide which effect combinations work best together. Both the style of music you play and how much you want to invest in pedals, processors, and patch cables will be determining factors in the elaborateness of your rig. It's not necessary to have a stockpile of these devices; while they're guaranteed to make you a more effected guitarist, they won't necessarily make you a better guitarist—unless the variety of sounds inspires your playing to the next level, which is quite possible!

Check out the following basic effect pedal rig, which is effective for a number of stylistic situations:

Basic Pedal Rig I

This setup would be good for someone who wants more variety than the standard overdrive or distorted amp tone. The ability to add chorus, flange, or phase to their effect arsenal is a nice touch, the compressor would help keep everything balanced and even-sounding, and you'd get a little added sustain to boot!

Here is another suggested pedal rig:

Basic Pedal Rig II

Rig II is ideal for someone seeking vintage tones (wah), tonal variety (overdrive/distortion), and a little added equalization for a frequency or lead boost.

Here are some suggested setups for selected musical styles:

Classic Guitar Effect Signal Chain

The classic guitar effect signal chain would also be good for rock and blues guitarists wanting minimal effects—nothing too far from the basics.

Wild Guitar Effect Signal Chain

The "wild guitar" rig has a bit more edge. It's actually a very common effect sequence. The wah and octave could be punched for an occasional treat, but the noise gate, modulation, and delay effects would probably be continually activated.

Balanced Guitar Effect Signal Chain

Using the balanced guitar setup is ideal for achieving a nice balance between tone shaping and useful effect changes.

What Not to Do

The possible combinations of effects are limitless, since there are so many options available on the market. Therefore, it's critical to know what won't work in a given effect sequence. Here are a couple of tips:

- Do not place reverb before other effects in a chain, as doing so will add reverb to every subsequent effect—which tends to sound unpleasant.
- Do not place overdrive and/or distortion at the end of the chain.

Now that you've been introduced to some useful effect arrangements, use these examples as catalysts for your own ideas. Listen to the impact a new effect has on your usual sound. Aside from any tonal benefits, listen for subtle changes such as additional noise, frequency changes, or colorization. Remember that anything and everything that you add to your arsenal will affect your overall sound.

Chapter 13
BUILDING A PEDALBOARD

In this chapter, we'll look at how to assemble an efficient and suitable pedalboard for your particular needs. Unless you're using only one or two pedals, you'll want to organize and house your effects, adapters, and cables within a compact and portable casing.

Choosing Your Pedalboard

There are several products on the market that serve as suitable pedalboards. However, although DOD and Boss offer products compatible with their own pedals, they impart little flexibility with non-proprietary devices (pedals from various manufactures often require different adapters and/or voltage specifications).

A popular pedalboard that is relatively inexpensive is made by SKB, which is widely known for its durable multi-spaced racks cases. The SKB PS-25 pedalboard features two separate effect loops, which allow you to seamlessly run your effects through two different amplifiers, and 9-volt outlets (with adapters) to power up to six pedals.

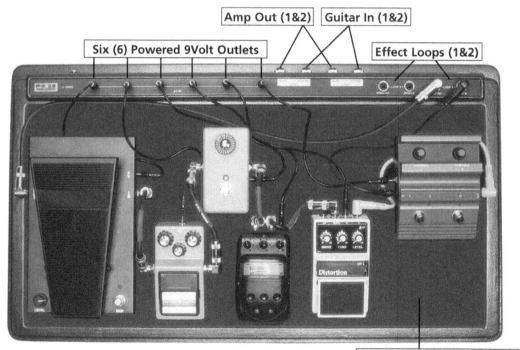

SKB PS-25 Powered Pedalboard

This pedalboard is perfect for the guitarist wanting to affix their pedals to a powered surface, which makes transporting to band practice and gigs less cumbersome.

Assembling Your Pedalboard

An important factor in assembling your pedalboard is dealing with instrument cables. If you plan to connect several pedals to your amplifier, you will need a stockpile of quality 1/4-inch cables. Several cable manufactures produce high-quality instrument cable, such as Monster, Horizon, and Pro Co.

Common 1/4-inch Instrument Cable

Cables such as the one pictured above are ideal for patching your guitar to your amplifier or pedalboard; but you may want (or need) to consider purchasing right-angled plugs, which more easily and effectively connect closely placed pedals together.

Right-Angled 1/4-inch Instrument Cable

If you're planning to put together a pedal rig using a pedalboard (such as the SKB PS-25), you will need at least two 15- to 20-foot 1/4-inch cables, in addition to several shorter 1/4-inch cables, for connecting the pedals to each other and to the pedalboard's effects loop.

Another useful pedal to consider when assembling your pedalboard is a channel switcher/selector, or ABY box. Several companies produce these pedals—such as Morely and Whirlwind—which, at the press of a footswitch, can be activated to run two different amplifiers separately or at the same time.

The following is an illustration of a standard channel selector.

Morely ABY Channel Selector

Channel switchers also allow you the option of connecting two different guitars to one amplifier, which is useful when performing live and want to switch guitars quickly (like when a string breaks, or if a differently tuned guitar is called for in the same song), without having to unplug from your amplifier.

Check out the following illustration, which shows you two common setups for an ABY box.

Two Common Setups for Channel Selectors:

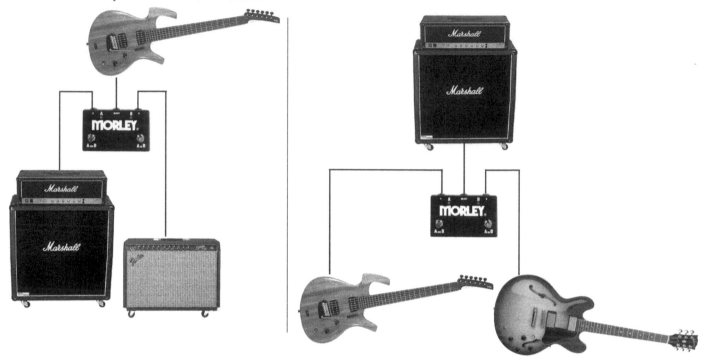

Completing the Connection of Your Pedalboard

Connecting the pedalboard to your amplifier is the final step of the assembly. Although you may choose to run some of your pedals into your amplifier's effect loop (if applicable), for simplicity's sake, you could also choose to connect your pedalboard directly into the input jack of your amp.

The following diagram demonstrates how to connect your guitar and amplifier to an SKB PS-25 pedalboard using the amp's input jack.

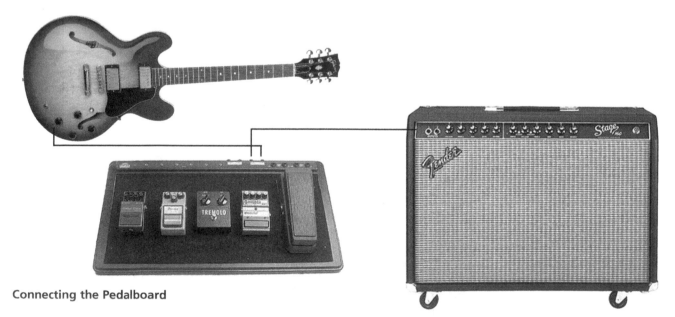

Connecting the Pedalboard

Once you have connected all of your pedals together and have them fully powered by the pedalboard, connect your guitar, then your amplifier to the pedalboard as well. The result is an efficient and professional-looking setup that saves floor space in cramped rehearsal spaces and performance stages. You're now ready to power everything up and play!

Chapter 14
MULTI-EFFECT PROCESSORS

Most of this book has focused on stomp boxes or foot pedals, but all of the suggestions and tone tips can be applied to multi-effect processors as well.

The world of multi-effect devices has flourished recently, as new brands and styles of all-in-one units are available from a variety of manufacturers. Some of the most popular units are from companies such as Boss, Line 6, Lexicon, DigiTech, Zoom, and Korg.

The premise behind multi-effect units is the capability of producing and manipulating a wide assortment of sounds from one device. Most of these processors have digital or LED menus that display the parameters and settings of the particular effects you are using. In many ways, these units are like having everything and the kitchen sink—they feature hundreds of tonal varieties and dozens of effects to choose from. The only problem with these processors is the making of selections and then setting them.

A common difficulty with multi-effects units is that inexperienced users can easily spend more time programming it than actually playing through it. But once you have created some sounds of your own and stored them into the memory, you should find that these units are invaluable.

Take a look at the following illustration, which shows a rack-mounted multi-effect device.

Lexicon Rack-Mounted Multi-Effects Unit

Some of the multi-effect units on the market are strictly effect processors, which means that they only produce modulation and time-based effects (i.e., chorus, flange, phase, delay, reverb, etc.). Also available are preamp/processors, which produce guitar tones—like an amplifier would—in addition to various guitar-related effects.

Deciding which multi-effect unit is right for you is crucial when buying new gear. Many of the processors out there are expensive, but there are also less costly processors that perform well and sound decent.

Assembling a Rack System

Rack systems for guitarists came into prominence during the mid 1980s, when legions of touring and studio guitarists needed a portable system capable of a variety of tones. Steve Lukather, David Gilmour, Steve Vai, and Mike Landau all requested the services of renowned rack-system builder Bob Bradshaw, whose high-dollar rack systems featured inventive and flexible tone selection. These units also incorporated the famous Bradshaw Switching System, which allowed guitarists to switch guitar tones, effect parameters, and foot pedals with a touch of a button.

The following illustration diagrams an assembly that includes guitar–preamp–power amp–cabinet connections.

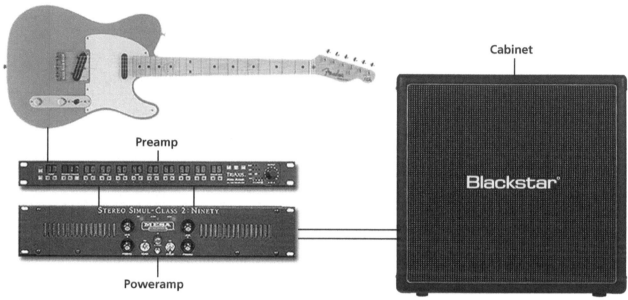

Connecting a Rack System

There are a variety of options to connecting gear like this—such as adding additional rack units, floor pedals, and footswitches. Normally, separate preamp units provide more sounds and tonal flavors than those self-contained within amplifiers, making such a setup the more expensive alternative. But the tonal variety and flexibility provided by separate pre-am/amp assemblies more than makes up for the added expense.

Floor-Based Units

Along with rack-mountable multi-effect processors, several manufacturers (Boss, DigiTech, Zoom, etc.) offer like devices designed as floor units. These units are perfect for the guitarist who already owns a good-sounding amplifier, desires a variety of effects and guitar tones, but doesn't want to invest in and assemble a rack system. Most are equipped with a wide assortment of effects, an onboard tuner, an expression pedal (for wah and volume effects), and memory banks for custom guitar tones.

The following illustration shows a basic floor-based multi-effect unit.

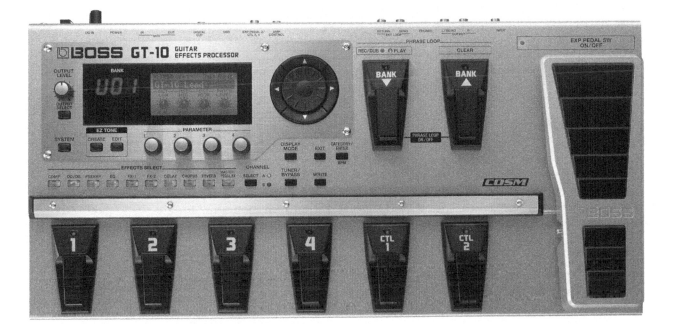

Boss GT-10 Guitar Effects Processor

Activated by a footswitch, the floor-based effect processors are useful for guitarists who want easy access to a variety of tones during live performances (no struggling with standard rack knobs and controls). It's also ideal for guitarists who don't want to deal with a pedalboard's multiple foot pedals, as this arsenal of different guitar effects is self-contained, easily accessible, and ready to use.

Your individual musical needs and sound variety requirements will determine whether a handful of foot pedals or a multi-effects processor is right for you. If you're just looking for a few new sounds to add to your tone, I suggest trying a few foot pedals to start. If you're certain that you would prefer to experiment with different effects and tone settings, then a multi-effects processor might be the better choice.

Do some research on the different brands and models available, and be sure to actually plug into some of these devices before you buy. You'll probably discover that some of these units sound radically different from one another, and may sound different yet through your particular amplifier.

Chapter 15
AMPLIFIER AND EFFECT MODELING

Amplifier and effect modeling has been around for over a decade. Modeling refers to products designed to replicate qualities of vintage sounds: those of tube amplifiers, analog effects, and the various characteristics of legendary guitar tones. The practice of modeling relies on advanced technology and computer-generated samples from the specific amplifier or effect that manufacture wants to emulate.

Amplifier Modeling
Modeling amps are all-in-one units capable of replicating a variety of vintage tones. The Line 6 Spider IV is one such amp, which modeled a number of classic amp tones (Fender, Marshall, Ibanez). While the notion may sound impressive (and many of these products actually do sound great), a sample tone taken from classic guitar amp will never truly replicate that of the original. Because there is a noticeable difference between the replicated tone and the original, many "tone purists" feel that these products are blasphemous.

The following illustrates two modeling amplifiers.

Common Modeling Amplifiers

Line 6 Spider IV Modeling Amp   **Peavey Vypyr100 Modeling Amp**

Effect Modeling
Effect modeling is becoming quite popular as well, not only for their modeling capabilities, but as stand-alone units. Companies such as Line 6 and Roland have released products that emulate the sounds of classic guitar effect pedals.

These products are based upon the same premise as the modeling amps, relying on computer-generated tone emulation to replicate the tonal characteristics of classic (and obsolete) stomp boxes and foot pedals.

If you are looking for a specific guitar effect or amplifier tone, effect modelers such as these can help you change the sound of your existing guitar amp without the expense of buying a complete modeling amplifier. Line 6 has produced several modeling pedals, which emulate classic delay, modulation, and distortion effects. The following are illustrations of Line 6 effect modeling pedals.

Effect Modeling Pedals

Line 6 DM4 Distortion Modeler Pedal

Line 6 DL4 Delay Guitar Effects Pedal

Roland also offers modeling products featuring COSM technology (Composite Object Sound Modeling), such as the GP-100 preamp/processor and the acclaimed VG-8. Both produce useful guitar tones combined with a plethora of effect-processing options.

The choice is yours: you could spend a great deal of time and several thousand dollars collecting an assortment of truly vintage amplifiers and effects, or you could spend minimal time and under a thousand dollars for near-replications of their classic tones.

Roland VGA7 V-Guitar Amplifier

Chapter 16
GETTING A GOOD TONE THROUGH YOUR PC

Personal computers and the Internet have changed the way the world functions technologically. For musicians, these conveniences have served as portals to new musical information, virtual guitar lessons, downloaded music, homemade tablature, and the opportunity to communicate with musicians around the globe.

More and more guitarists are plugging their electric guitars into computers via sound cards; and thanks to several amplifier and effect companies, they're finally able to get some good tones through average PCs with only mediocre speaker systems.

The following is a step-by-step overview of how to get the best sound from your personal computer.

Step 1—Plugging In
What do you want from your PC? If you want a basic, clean, dry tone with no overdrive or effects, you can plug your guitar directly into your sound card using a 1/4- to 1/8-inch shielded instrument cable. If you already have a 1/4-inch instrument cable that you'd like to use instead, you can purchase a 1/8-inch adapter, and plug one end of it into your sound card.

NOTE: Be careful that you don't damage your PC speakers by turning your guitar and computer speakers up too high. Remember that your computer's speakers are a lot smaller than those in your amp.

Step 2—Listen Carefully
Once you have connected your guitar (and pedals, if desired), you can monitor your guitar's sound through your computer as long *as you're sure that the sound card is in perfect operating condition*. Your guitar will sound much different than it does through your amplifier, but at least you are now able to play your guitar through your PC speakers.

If you are content with the way your guitar sounds, then you are finished with this chapter. Otherwise, keep reading!

Step 3—Sound Advice
If you are unsatisfied with the guitar tone you're getting through your PC speakers, there are a couple of things that you could try:

- **Upgrade your computer's sound card.** This may seem a bit excessive if all you want to do is play your guitar through your computer speakers, but in many cases this will greatly improve the tone as processed through your PC. An added bonus is that an upgraded sound card will enhance any recording or MP3 software, video game audio, and your overall PC audio.

- **Purchase a computer-compatible amplifier.** Such as Line 6's POD or Johnson's J-Station. These products are stand-alone preamp/processors that are excellent for various musical situations—recording, live performance, band rehearsal, home practice—but they also sound great when connected to a computer's sound card.

Computer-Compatible Guitar Amplifiers

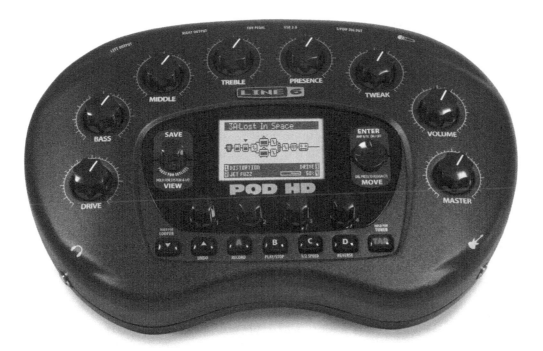

Line 6 POD HD Desktop Modeler

NOTE: All of the audio examples for this book were recorded on my computer!

Chapter 17
STYLISTIC GUITAR TONES

Finding the right sound for a particular style of music is important to any musician. For example, most blues guitarists do not play through rigs more suitable to a metal guitarist, because their stylistic tones are dissimilar enough to cause musical confusion. I'm not suggesting that experimentation, sound exploration, or defying expectation is a bad thing; I'm just saying that certain styles and tones are traditional and customary to particular genres.

The point here is this: it doesn't matter what type of guitar, amp, or effects you are using in your rig. What does matter is that you understand the genre and the contributions (sounds and styles, tones and effects) to the genre as made by guitarists of yesterday through today. A knowledge and appreciation of these things will help you to not only lend to the musical tradition, but to develop a sound of your own.

At this point in your tonal training, I feel that it is important for you to understand the guitar tones and sounds fundamental to particular styles. The following is an overview, complete with audio examples, of tones intrinsic to select genres.

Pop/Rock Tone

TRACK 21

Notice that outside of a small amount of overdrive—which adds edge to the strummed progression—the overall guitar tone featured on audio track 21 is dry with virtually no effects. This tone is evidence that, just because you have access to a stockpile of chorus, delays, harmonizers, and other effects, doesn't mean you have to use them all the time. Sometimes the best use of an effect is to keep it out of your mix.

Listen to some rock and pop tunes and compare their sounds with that coming out of your amplifier. Try adjusting your rig to replicate these tones. Can you identify which, if any effects, you'd need to incorporate to get closer to the pop and rock tones?

Metal Tone

TRACK 22

Listen to audio track 22 to hear a solid metal guitar tone—brutal-sounding with distortion. Notice also that the mid-range frequencies have been reduced, which is a primary difference between rock and metal guitar tones.

If you are unable to acquire a tone similar to that heard on the audio track, either an EQ or a pedal geared for metal distortion may be a device you should consider adding to your rig. If you are using an effect processor, try adding massive amounts of distortion; also, set the mid-range frequencies lower to get that characteristic "scooped-mid" metal sound.

Funk Tone

TRACK 23

Funk guitar purists normally have one tone in mind when scratching out ninth chords over a groove: that smooth-funk sound as attained by funk legend James Brown's guitarist Jimmy Nolen. Audio track 23 features an example of this type of tone.

Although there are currently many hybrids and mutations of the traditional funk style, most can be traced back to masters like James Brown, Sly and the Family Stone, and Parliament. Newer funk/rock artists like The Red Hot Chili Peppers and Lenny Kravitz have borrowed from the classic funk style created decades before them. Listen to some of the classic funk guitarists, then listen for their influence in the works of contemporary musicians. Try to replicate both styles and sounds.

Blues Tone

Blues guitarists traditionally adhere to clean or only slightly overdriven guitar tones. Guitar greats such as B.B. King, Muddy Waters, Albert King, and Albert Collins likewise favored the slight overdrive, but on some occasions cranked it up or added other effects.

Listen to audio track 24 for a sample blues tone.

TRACK 24

Modern blues guitarists such as Derek Trucks, Susan Tedeschi, and Kenny Wayne Sheppard maintain the traditional blues style, but have updated the genre with tones featuring more overdrive, more compression, more chorus. Listen to music from both the old and new schools, and try to attain the sounds used by both.

Jazz Tone

Traditional jazz guitarists prefer the sound produced by a hollowbody or semi-hollowbody guitar and an EQ setting for warm and bassy. You'll notice a near absence of effects on audio track 25, as their use within traditional jazz is minimal—the desired tone is attained with fingers, rather than a processor. Jazz legends such as Wes Montgomery, Charlie Christian, and Joe Pass rarely effected their guitar tones.

TRACK 25

Modern jazz/fusion guitarists like Scott Henderson, John Scofield, Mike Stern, and Pat Metheny each have their own approach to playing jazz music, and have their own signature sounds, employing various pedals, processors, and even guitar synthesizers in their individual guitar rigs.

Country Tone

The range of sounds country guitarists have used over the years is wide and varied: from the clean and smooth sounds of the legends like Chet Atkins, Jerry Reed, and Roy Clark, to the modern sounds of players like Jerry Donahue, Brent Mason, Dan Huff, and Brad Paisley. Country guitarists are known to use various effects for their guitar tones.

TRACK 26

One of the most recognizable country tones—the snappy Telecaster twang—is attained with an echo effect blended with a compressed, clean tone. If you don't have an actual Tele, try manipulating your effect to get this sound.

Surf Guitar Tone

Legend Dick Dale was the pioneer of surf guitar sound, which is actually a blend of many styles: rock, blues, rockabilly, and country. To achieve the authentic surf tone, you'll probably need an old-school tube amp, vibrato, tremolo, slap-back delay, tons of reverb, and a "spanky" Strat.

Listen to audio track 27 to hear the surf guitar sound. Also, watch *Pulp Fiction*—its soundtrack features the music of surf master Dick Dale.

TRACK 27

Chapter 18
FAMOUS EFFECTED GUITARISTS

In this final chapter, we'll take a look at the rigs responsible for some of the most recognizable and memorable guitar tones in musical history, and the guitarists that created them. All have greatly influenced how guitarists everywhere set up and dial in their own guitar tones.

Eric Clapton

As is evidenced from his earliest recordings with John Mayall and The Yardbirds, Eric Clapton knew how to dial in that captivating "woman tone"—full bodied and seductive.

Clapton's sound can be reproduced by simply rolling back the tone knob on your guitar until the treble (high-end) frequencies are reduced. If you have tone knobs that feature a number sequence, roll to about 7 or 8. This should cut slightly the higher frequencies and maintain much of your original tone.

Many tone aficionados would claim that Clapton's 1960s Cream compositions included some of the best rock tones ever produced. Here is an illustration of the Clapton's Cream-era rig.

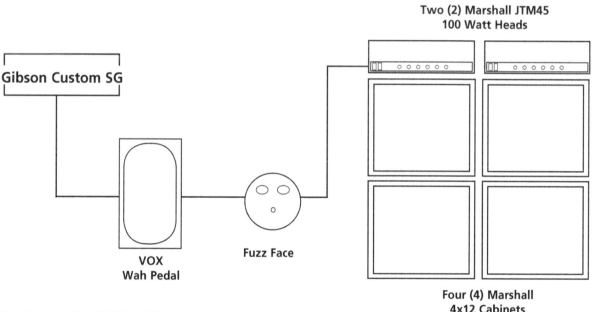

Eric Clapton Rig (1966–1968)

Although the diagram indicates the use of a custom Gibson SG with this rig, Clapton also used Les Paul Standards, Firebirds, and an ES-335 semi-hollowbody electric in order to get a greater variety of tones.

Jimi Hendrix

James Marshall Hendrix is surely one of the most revered and most famous rock guitarists of all time. It is a testament to his greatness that, considering his relatively short-lived career, his music continues to influence millions of guitarists the world over.

Although the guitar, amp, and effect options that were at his disposal in the 1960s were limited compared to those of today, Jimi still managed to shape a tone so innovative and exciting and that it inspired the subsequent sounds of icons like Eric Clapton, Stevie Ray Vaughan, and Steve Vai.

The following illustrates Jimi's setup.

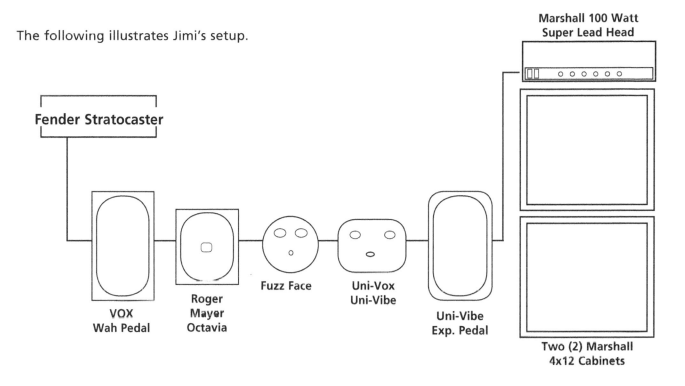

Jimi Hendrix Rig (1968–1970)

Eric Johnson

Rock-jazz guitarist Eric Johnson is a guitar player's guitar player. Often compared to giants such as Stevie Ray Vaughan, Pat Metheny, and Steve Morse, Johnson's brilliant technique is sonically enhanced by his unique and luscious violin-like tone.

To attain Eric's rich, liquid-like overdrive tone, incorporate a fuzz box for distortion and a Chandler Tube Driver for added sustain. Johnson's rig also includes two amps— through which his signal is split via a stereo chorus—which gives him that big, wide sound.

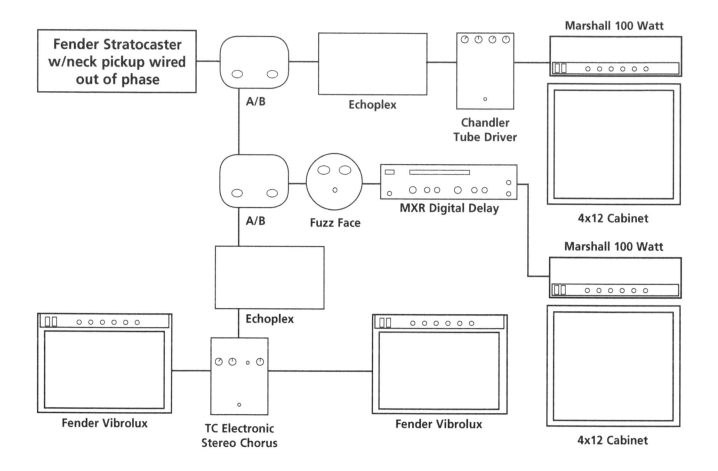

Pat Metheny

A jazz player with an untraditionally effected sound, Pat Metheny is a guitarist whose respectful approach to the genre's evolution has made him an icon among even the staunchest jazz purists. Versatile and innovative, Metheny favors a tone abundant with chorus and delay, but free of distortion.

The following illustrates Pat's setup, which includes compression and is run in stereo. Make sure to use a clean setting on your amp.

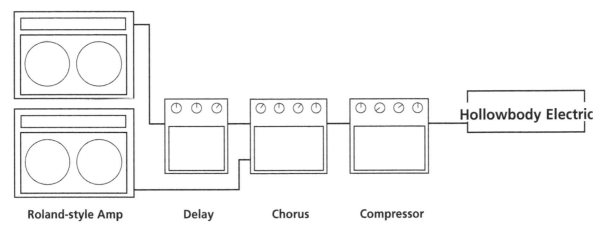

| Roland-style Amp | Delay | Chorus | Compressor | Hollowbody Electric |

Pat Methany Rig (Current)

Tom Morello

The unique sound and effects prowess of Rage Against The Machine's guitarist Tom Morello has garnered him a lot of respect since the band first burst onto the scene in the early 1990s. Sometimes furious and distorted, and other times cleanly overdriven and funky, Morello's sound proves his giftedness with guitar tone.

His colorful palate of effects, and his artistry for manipulating them, have helped him create not only modern funk-metal tones, but bizarre, ambient noises, scratching-record effects, and otherworldly sonics. So adept is he with guitar sounds that it's hard to believe they're not the product of a keyboard or non-guitar instrument; but RATM never used such devices.

The following is the layout that Tom used for RATM's self-titled debut album and corresponding tour.

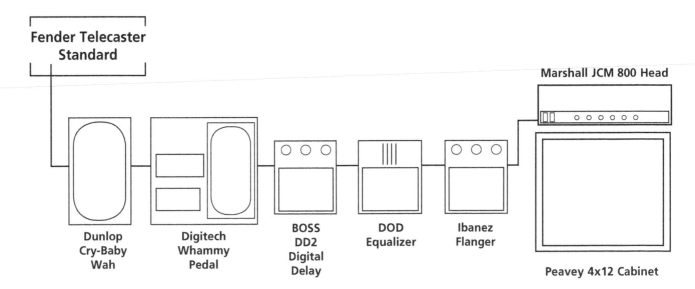

Fender Telecaster Standard — Dunlop Cry-Baby Wah — Digitech Whammy Pedal — BOSS DD2 Digital Delay — DOD Equalizer — Ibanez Flanger — Marshall JCM 800 Head — Peavey 4x12 Cabinet

Tom Morello Rig (1992)

Andy Summers

Known for his creative use of effects, Andy Summers was the man behind the shimmering, chorus-rich guitar tone of the Police. His Police-era rig, as illustrated below, included separate delays placed after the chorus, which yielded the mathematically precise bouncing of sound between left and right speakers.

Also incorporating compression and overdrive (just enough to get a warm distortion), Summers's tone also required signal splitting through the chorus and delays.

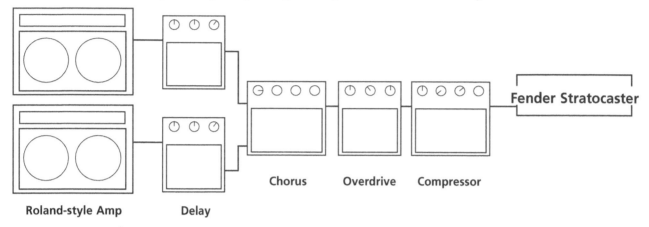

Roland-style Amp   Delay   Chorus   Overdrive   Compressor   Fender Stratocaster

Andy Summers Rig (Police Era)

Eddie Van Halen

Another important and highly influential guitarist is Eddie Van Halen, who burst onto the scene in the late 1970s. His novel techniques, flawless dexterity, and signature "brown sound" guitar tone impressed not only guitarists of rock, but of other idioms as well.

Eddie's early rig was comprised of equipment collected from his experimentations with sound. His guitars from this era he hand-assembled himself, trying many unique constructions and elaborations to acquire his own signature sound.

At the time of Van Halen's first album and tour in 1978, Eddie's amplifier of choice was a Marshall head and cabinets, and his pedalboard was literally attached to a 2" x 4" (which was, evidently, the object of ridicule by some of the big-name guitarists of the time; but once Eddie plugged in and played, the laughing undoubtedly stopped).

Here is Eddie's early setup, which is very similar to the rig he used for recording and touring during the first Van Halen album.

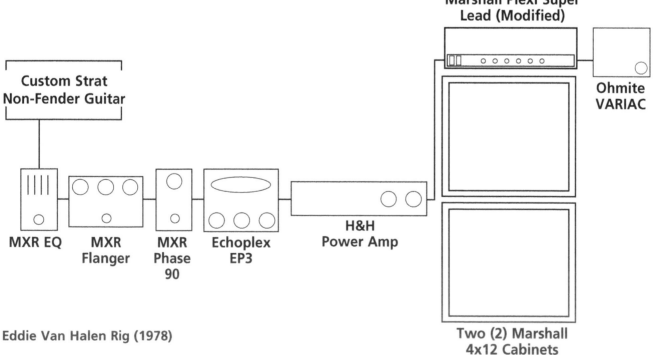

Marshall Plexi Super
Lead (Modified)

Custom Strat
Non-Fender Guitar

Ohmite
VARIAC

MXR EQ   MXR   MXR   Echoplex   H&H
          Flanger   Phase   EP3   Power Amp
                     90

Two (2) Marshall
4x12 Cabinets

Eddie Van Halen Rig (1978)

Stevie Ray Vaughan

In many ways, Stevie Ray Vaughan helped keep the blues alive during the early 1980s, when the genre hit a rough period commercially, as many blues musicians' albums and concerts were selling poorly. But once this immortal legend shook things up, the blues experienced a resurgence of popularity and esteem.

During his short career, the secret to Vaughan's guitar tone eluded many guitarists wanting to capture his sound. Even today, the mystery behind his massive guitar tone still exists. It is known, however, that Stevie used heavy gauge strings, various foot pedals, and old tube amplifiers.

Stevie was also known to play loudly, both on recordings and during live performances, but most of his tone came straight from his fingers. (The tone that guitarists get from their fingers will affect their overall sound—the touch and attack of the strings make a difference.)

Here is SRV's layout as used in the studio and on tour in the mid-1980s.

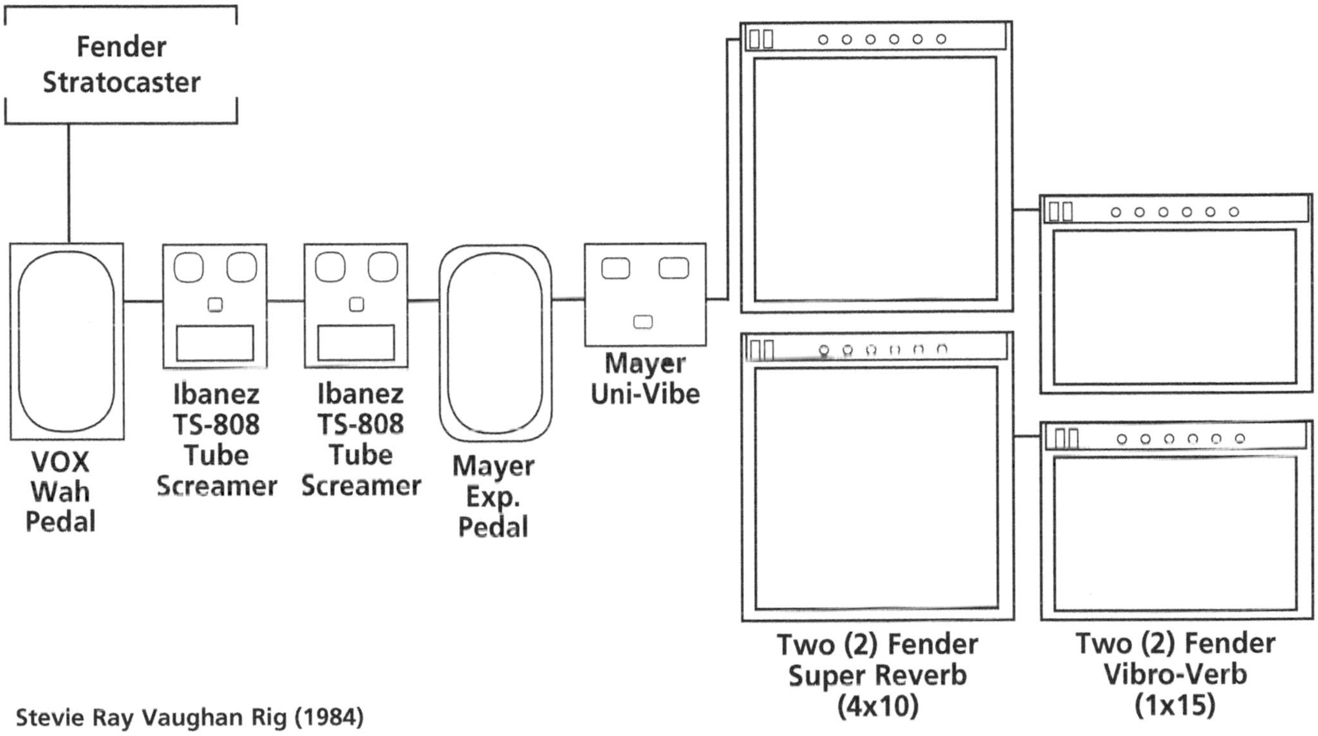

Stevie Ray Vaughan Rig (1984)

Vaughan changed his rig often, and the setup shown here changed dramatically by the end of his career. When playing live, he would occasionally augment the featured layout with various pedals, amps, and guitars.

Appendix:
Effected Guitar Music

The following is a list of effected music according to effect type:

Overdrive
Stevie Ray Vaughan, "Texas Flood"
Jimi Hendrix, "Bold as Love"
ZZ Top, "La Grange"
Led Zeppelin, "Good Times, Bad Times"
James Gang, "Funk #49"

Delay
Van Halen, "Cathedral"
Pink Floyd, "Run Like Hell"
The Police, "Walking on the Moon"
Extreme, "Flight of the Wounded Bumblebee"
Eric Johnson, "SRV"

Distortion
Metallica, "The Thing That Should Not Be"
Metallica, "Enter Sandman"
Pantera, "By Demons Be Driven"
Soundgarden, "Spoonman"
Stone Temple Pilots, "Wicked Garden"

Octave
Jimi Hendrix, "Purple Haze" (Solo)
Jimi Hendrix, "Fire" (Solo)
Jimi Hendrix, "Machine Gun"
Led Zeppelin, "Fool in the Rain"
Soundgarden, "Rusty Cage"

Fuzz
Jimi Hendrix, "Foxy Lady"
Cream, "Sunshine of Your Love"
Led Zeppelin, "Whole Lotta Love" (Solo)
Santana, "Black Magic Woman"
ZZ Top, "36–24–36"

Harmonizer
Steve Vai, "Answers"
Steve Vai, "Ballerina 12/24"
Yes, "Owner of a Lonely Heart" (Solo)
Rush, Closer to the Heart" (Solo)
Buckethead, "Jowls" (Intro)

Chorus
Rush, "Red Barchetta"
Joe Satriani, "Always with You, Always with Me"
John Scofield, "Blue Matter"
Pat Metheny, "Phase Dance"
Living Colour, "Open Letter (To a Landlord)

Wah
Jimi Hendrix, "Voodoo Chile (Slight Return)"
Cream, "White Room"
Funkadelic, "Maggot Brain"
Robin Trower, "Too Rolling Stoned"
Joe Satriani, "Surfing with the Alien"

Phaser
Van Halen, "Atomic Punk"
Van Halen, "Ain't Talkin' 'Bout Love"
Rush, "The Spirit of the Radio"
Rage Against The Machine, "People of the Sun"
Red Hot Chili Peppers, "Blood Sugar Sex Magik"

Talk Box
Peter Frampton, "Do You Feel Like I Do?"
Joe Walsh, "Rocky Mountain Way"
Jeff Beck, "She's a Woman"
Nazareth, "Hair of the Dog"
Pink Floyd, "What Do You Want from Me?"

Flanger
Van Halen, "Unchained"
Van Halen, "Hear About It Later"
Heart, "Barracuda"
Led Zeppelin, "Nobody's Fault But Mine"
Incubus, "I Miss You"

Pitch Shifting
Pantera, "Cemetery Gates"
Rage Against The Machine, "Killing in the Name Of"
Rage Against The Machine, "Bulls on Parade"
Joe Satriani, "Raspberry Jam Delta"
Living Colour, "Ignorance Is Bliss"

Tremolo / Vibrato
Pink Floyd, "Money"
Nirvana, "Smells Like Teen Spirit"
Incubus, "The Warmth"
Robin Trower, "Bridge of Sighs"
Led Zeppelin, "Dazed and Confused"

Wild Effects
Jimi Hendrix, "Are You Experienced?"
Steve Vai, "Alien Water Kiss"
Buckethead, "Night of the Slunk"
Eric Johnson, "Ah Via Musicom"
Rage Against The Machine, "Vietnow"

Reverb
Jeff Beck, "Where Were You?"
Jimi Hendrix, "All Along the Watchtower"
Joe Walsh, "Turn to Stone"
Pat Metheny, "San Lorenzo"
Rush, "Distant Early Warning"

BOOKS ABOUT GUITARS

The Beauty of the 'Burst
Gibson Sunburst Les Pauls from '58 to '60

by Yasuhiko Iwanade • Hal Leonard

The Beauty of the 'Burst pays tribute to Gibson's magnificent Sunburst Les Pauls made between 1958 and 1960, the most highly prized solidbody electric guitars ever. The book features lavish full-color photos of these beautiful instruments throughout; the guitars of famous players; a foreword by Ted McCarty; a bio of the author, world renowned collector Yasuhiko Iwanade; and the "Science of the Burst" section with over 30 pages of detailed reference facts on every facet of the guitar, including colors, wood figure, pick-ups, hardware and qualities of "voice."

00330265.. **$34.99**

9780793573745

The Dream Factory
Fender Custom Shop

by Tom Wheeler • Hal Leonard
Foreword by Billy F. Gibbons

This third in a series of hardcover books joins the award-winning titles *The Stratocaster Chronicles* and *The Soul of Tone* by author/historian Tom Wheeler. In nearly 600 pages, *The Dream Factory* features hundreds of full-color photos of incredibly rare, collectible, and limited-edition handcrafted guitars. Learn how the Fender Custom Shop, originally intended to employ just two master craftsmen, grew into the most prolific custom instrument shop in the music industry.

00331976.. **$75.00**

9781423436980

The Epiphone Guitar Book
A Complete History of Epiphone Guitars

by Walter Carter • Backbeat Books

The story of Epiphone, one of the oldest and most famous guitar companies, is told by former staff historian Walter Carter. It's an epic story spanning three centuries, from Old World roots in the 19th century to the golden age of American makers in the 20th century and onward into the global market of the new millennium. Beautifully illustrated with photos of all the important Epiphone instruments and the extraordinary musicians who played them, this is a fascinating history of an iconic name in the world of the guitar.

00333269 .... **$27.99**

9781617130977

The Fender Bass
An Illustrated History

by J.W. Black and Albert Molinaro
Hal Leonard

When Leo Fender added a bass to his growing family of instruments 50 years ago, he created a new world for musicians and revolutionized an industry in the process. Using hundreds of photographs, this exciting release chronicles the evolution of that instrument from 1951 to 2001, providing background, history and highly researched facts vital to understanding everything about this remarkable member of the Fender family. A must for all music fans!

00330755.. **$24.99**

The Fender Electric Guitar Book – 3rd Edition
A Complete History of Fender Instruments

by Tony Bacon • Backbeat Books

Fender guitars have long been the instruments of choice for arti sts such as Jeff Beck, Eric Clapton, Jimi Hendrix and Stevie Ray Vaughan. This book tells the complete story of Fender guitars, detailing classics such as the Telecaster, Stratocaster & Jazzmaster as well as lesser-known models. Dozens of photos reveal Fender's storied craftsmanship, while the text includes collector details for all models. The reference section lists all models and their statistics.

00331752.. **$24.95**

9780879308971

The Fender Telecaster
by A.R. Duchossoir • Hal Leonard

The Fender Telecaster is regarded as the first commercially successful solid body electric 'Spanish' guitar. Designed by Leo Fender at a time when the words rock and roll were not even coined, the 'Telly' is the senior member of a family of instruments whose sounds and looks helped revolutionize the world of popular music. This book relates the story of Telecaster Guitars since 1950—everything you ever wanted to know is explored through lots of color and black and white photos, charts and interviews.

00183003.. **$16.99**

9780793508600

The Other Brands of Gibson
by Paul Fox • Centerstream Publications

From 1929 through 1961 Gibson, Inc. of Kalamazoo, MI produced over 30 brands of musical instruments that did not carry the Gibson name. Many of these brands may be familiar, with names such as Recording King, National and Washburn, while many others are brands that only a handful of avid Gibsonites will know, such as Werlein Leader, Grinnell, Truett, and many more. This book is a complete guide to all of the other brands Gibson produced, complete with detailed descriptions, photos and rare examples of existing instruments from collectors around the world.

00001560 .... **$29.99**

9781574242713

50 Years of Gretsch Electrics
by Tony Bacon • Backbeat Books

Introduced in 1954 as one of Gretsch's "Guitars of the Future," the White Falcon was an overwhelmingly impressive instrument. The influence of this spectacular new guitar spread to other models and guitar manufacturers. This book compiles the best of Gretsch's inventions over the past 50 years and tells the stories of their creation and the men who created them. Includes 100 photos!

00331258 .... **$27.99**

9780879308223

The Gretsch Electric Guitar Book
60 Years of White Falcons, 6120s, Jets, Gents, and More
by Tony Bacon • Backbeat Books
The Gretsch Electric Guitar Book comes right up to the present, including Gretsch's alliance to the powerful Fender company, a move that has done wonders for the reliability and playability of the modern Gretsch axe. Tony Bacon's updated and revised story of Gretsch is three great volumes in one: a compendium of luscious pictures of the coolest guitars; a gripping story from early exploits to the most recent developments; and a detailed collector's guide to every production electric Gretsch model ever made.
00120793 ....$29.99
9781480399242

The Guitar Player Repair Guide – 3rd Revised Edition
by Dan Erlewine • Backbeat Books
This expanded edition for beginners to experts is a step-by-step manual to maintaining and repairing electric and acoustic guitars and basses. Players learn how to set up a guitar and keep it in top form by mastering basic maintenance. Features an essential DVD that makes guitar maintenance easier than ever. New features include set-up specs of leading players; stronger coverage of guitar electronics, including pickups and wiring diagrams; and expanded coverage of acoustics.
00331793 Book/DVD Pack $34.99
9780879309213

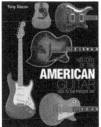

History of the American Guitar
1833 to the Present Day
by Tony Bacon • Backbeat Books
History of the American Guitar begins in New York City in the 1830s with the arrival of Christian Martin, from Germany, to set up the Martin company. Over 75 brand names are represented, with more than 300 guitars photographed in stunning detail, including Bigsby, Danelectro, D'Angelico, D'Aquisto, Ditson, Dobro, Dyer, Epiphone, Fender, Gibson, Gretsch, James Trussart, Kay, Maccaferri, Martin, Micro-Frets, Mosrite, Oahu, Ovation, Regal, Rickenbacker, Stromberg, Taylor, Vega, Wilkanowski, and many more.
00333186 ....$29.99
09781617130335

How to Make Your Electric Guitar Play Great!
Second Edition
by Dan Erlewine
Backbeat Books
From shopping for a first electric guitar to setting customized action, this do-it-yourself primer for owning and maintaining an electric guitar explains the ins and outs of choosing the right guitar; cleaning, tools, and basic maintenance; personalizing and improving on a "factory setup;" troubleshooting; basic guitar electronics; choosing and installing replacement pickups, and capacitors; setups of the pros; and much more. This new edition is overhauled from top to bottom and re-organized to make it easy for the reader to make his electric guitar sound and play great.
00333024 Book/Online Video $29.99
9780879309985

Martin Guitars: A History
by Richard Johnston and Dick Boak
Hal Leonard
Part of a two-book set, *The History: Book 1* covers the people, the places, and the stories of an American icon. Richly illustrated, this book covers the story right up to the fifth-generation president Chris Martin IV. Because the original and revision authors had complete access to authorized archives, this version is the most accurate and detailed reference on the topic. Leading up to the re-vitalization of the 1990s and the remarkable sustenance of its legacy, hundreds of photographs and documents effectively show the people and the guitars that made the company famous.
00330889 ....$32.00
9780634037856

Martin Guitars: A Technical Reference
by Richard Johnston and Dick Boak
Hal Leonard
Part of a two book set, this book provides information on guitar bodies, necks, headstocks, bridges, woods, as well as other chapters covering Models by Style, the Custom Shop and limited editions. All the lesser known instruments like archtops, electrics, mandolins and ukuleles are included as well, all very collectible. The book ends with exhaustive appendices covering production numbers, retail prices, and instrument specifications.
00331986..$45.00
9781423439820

The PRS Electric Guitar Book
A Complete History of Paul Reed Smith Electrics Revised and Updated Edition
by Dave Burrluck • Backbeat Books
This book examines every part of PRS history, with an in-depth story, beautiful photographs, and detailed collector's info. Paul Reed Smith set up his first PRS factory in 1985 in Maryland and has devised guitars from the regular Custom and McCarty models, through the outrageously decorated Dragon specials and the controversial Singlecut, and on to recent achievements such as the Mira, Dave Grissom DGT, JA-15, and the S2 models. Dozens of guitars are pictured inside along with players, ads, catalogs, and rare memorabilia.
00120792..$29.99
9781480386273

Spann's Guide to Gibson 1902-1941
by Joe Spann
Centerstream Publications
Centerstream presents this detailed look at the inner workings of the famous musical instrument manufacturer of Kalamazoo, Michigan before World War II. For the first time, Gibson fans can learn about the employees who built the instruments, exactly where the raw materials came from, the identity of parts vendors, and how the production was carried out. The book explains Gibson's pre-World War II factory order number and serial number systems, and corrects longstanding chronological errors.
00001525..$39.99
9781574242676

The Telecaster Guitar Book
A Complete History of Fender Telecaster Guitars Revised and Updated
by Tony Bacon
Backbeat Books
The Tele is the longest-lived solidbody electric, played by everyone from Muddy Waters to Keith Richards, from Radiohead to Snow Patrol. Its sheer simplicity and versatility are vividly illustrated here through interviews with Jeff Beck, James Burton, Bill Kirchen, John 5, and more. The book is three great volumes in one: a compendium of luscious pictures of the most desirable Teles, a gripping story from the earliest days to the latest exploits, and a detailed collector's guide to every Tele ever made.
00333189 ....$24.99
9781617131059

HAL•LEONARD®

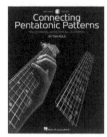
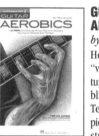

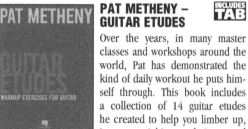

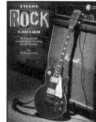